Natural Christmas Crafts

Ilona Butterer

STACKPOLE
BOOKS

Contents

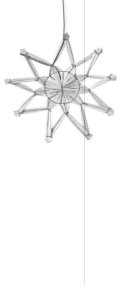

Foreword

The days are getting shorter, the nights are darker, and the year is slowly coming to a close. It is a time for cozy evenings, storytelling, and warm candlelight. We decorate our homes and prepare everything for a Christmas celebration where the family can come together and remember what is truly important.

Especially in the winter, I like to decorate with natural materials. I walk outdoors and collect various items, I find inspiration in the amazing shapes of various spices, and I enjoy the lasting green of the pine branches. I combine these found objects with paper, felt, raffia, and other natural materials to create one-of-a-kind decorations. Let yourself be inspired by the decorating ideas in this book, and discover the natural elegance of using materials from nature during the Christmas season.

Best wishes,

Ilana Butterer

The most wonderful time of the year

creative candleholders from recycled materials

Total height

approx. 20 in. (50 cm)

Materials

- Empty bottles in decorative shapes (labels removed)

- Straw stars in various sizes

- Red-and-white yarn

- Matte white spray paint

- Wooden stick

- Red candles in the appropriate sizes

- Wooden numbers: 1, 2, 3, and 4 (if desired)

Find four glass bottles in a variety of shapes. Wine and champagne bottles are especially good for this project. Apply two to three coats of spray paint to the bottles. An easy way to apply the paint: Put the bottle on the end of a stick. If you can't paint it outside, set up a large cardboard box and hold the bottle inside the box as you apply the spray paint to keep the spray under control. Always make sure to open a window for ventilation. To dry the bottle, prop the stick upright with the bottle on it, in a cinderblock, for instance.

Once the paint is dry, you can use the multicolored yarn to tie the straw stars to the bottles, and then stick the candles into the bottle openings. You may need to whittle down the end of the candles a bit so that they fit into the openings.

This decoration also works well with many other accessories. I happened to fall in love with these wooden numbers. What about you?

Straw stars are traditional German Christmas decorations. The straw represents the manger where Jesus was laid after his birth, and the star is a symbol of hope. With a little practice, you can make your own straw stars. But of course it's faster to buy them at a specialty store or a Christmas craft sale.

Wintry hurricane lamps

with grapevines and birchbark

Total height

approx. 6 in. (15 cm)

Materials

- Whitewashed grapevine wreath, 12 in. (30 cm) in diameter

- Glass cylinder, 6 in. (15 cm) in diameter, 6 in. (15 cm) tall

- Birchbark stars, 1¾ in. (4.5 cm) in diameter

- Iridescent faceted glass beads in light green, light blue, and plum

- 28-gauge (0.3 mm) silver wire

- Straight pins, ¾ in. (18 mm) long

- Short white pillar candle, 4 in. (10 cm) in diameter, 4 in. (10 cm) tall

First, place the glass cylinder with the candle in the middle of the wreath.

With each pin, attach one bead and one birchbark star to the wreath. You can place the stars randomly or in a spiral all the way around the wreath, as shown here, from the bottom to the top.

If you can find birchbark sheets, you can cut out your own stars. Or cut them out of patterned paper.

Thread a few of the faceted glass beads onto the silver wire and wrap it around the middle of the glass four or five times. Twist the ends of the wire together. Make sure the wire is tight enough that it stays where you want it.

Finally, move the beads around on the wire and arrange them decoratively.

Birchbark is a very attractive material. Its light wood and fairly subtle patterns make it the perfect backdrop for many different design ideas. In addition, birch has a lovely symbolic meaning that fits well with the Christmas season: It is the tree of love, life, and happiness.

A garden view

winter stillness sets in

Total height

approx. 36 in. (90 cm)

Materials

- Decorative flowerpot, 6 in. (15 cm) in diameter, 6 in. (15 cm) tall

- Delicate twigs

- Florist's foam

- Dry leaves or similar for covering the foam

- 3 yd. (2.7 m) wine-colored jute ribbon, 1½ in. (4 cm) wide

- Miniature wooden clothes-pins, 1 in. (2.5 cm) long

- 2 pieces of stiff decorative paper with complementary patterns

- Craft knife and cutting mat

- Kitchen knife for cutting the foam to size

Pattern

Page 60

Fill the pot with the florist's foam. Generally, this foam comes in a block and can be cut to fit your pot with a normal kitchen knife. Fill in gaps around the edges with smaller pieces of foam. It is important to fill up the pot as completely as possible.

Cut the ends of the twigs on a diagonal to form a point, then place them as close together as possible around the edge of the pot, pushing them into the foam. Cover the foam surface with the dry leaves or a suitable alternative,

like moss. Weave two pieces of jute ribbon through the twigs and tie the ends together.

Use the templates (page 60) to cut out several birds from the decorative paper, using paper with a different pattern for the wings. Glue the wings to the body with craft glue. If you like, you can curl the wings gently before gluing them on so that they stand out from the body a little bit. Attach the finished birds to the twigs, using the wooden clothespins.

This idea can be used to decorate your home or garden year-round, not just at Christmas. In the fall, for instance, when the first leaves start to turn, or in the spring when the birds return from their winter homes, this decoration is an attractive eye-catcher and can reflect the season depending on the colors you choose.

Falling stars

a rustic and playful candle display

Total height

approx. 18 in. (46 cm)

Materials

- Weathered wooden block, approx. 4 by 5 in. (10 by 13 cm), 7 in. (18 cm) tall

- Slice of birch wood, 3 in. (8 cm) in diameter

- White pillar candle, 2¼ in. (6 cm) in diameter, 5 in. (13 cm) tall

- Wire star, 12 in. (30 cm) in diameter

- 3 red felt stars, 2 in. (5 cm) in diameter

- 2 wire stars made of red painted wire

- Red-and-white yarn

- 2 yd. (1.8 m) red-and-white plaid ribbon with wire edging, 1½ in. (4 cm) wide

- Double-sided foam adhesive strip, 1/10 in. (3 mm) thick

- Hot glue

- Scissors

Tie the plaid ribbon around the wooden block as if it were a present, and make a decorative bow. Cut off the ends of the ribbon nicely. If you are using a larger piece of wood, the ribbon will need to be longer.

Attach the large wire star to the upper right and left edges of the block, slightly toward the back, using hot glue. For added stability, cut grooves in the edges of the block where the bottom edges of the star will fall. Use the yarn to hang two of the felt stars and the red wire stars from one arm of the large wire star. Tie the last felt star onto the other side of the large star

Attach the slice of birch wood to the center of the block, using the foam adhesive strip, and place the candle on it.

Festive pinecone tree

simple elegance

Total height

approx. 16 in. (40 cm)

Materials

- 2 round firewood logs, approx. 10 in. (25 cm) tall

- 2 pinecones, approx. 6 in. (15 cm) tall

- A few twigs, approx. 8 in. (20 cm) long

- 2 shell buttons or disks, 2 in. (5 cm) in diameter

- Star-shaped craft hole punch, approx. 1¼ in. (3 cm) wide

- White glitter paper

- 3 yd. (2.7 m) white wool felt ribbon, ⅝ in. (15 mm) wide, cut into two pieces

- 14-gauge (1.6 mm) metal wire

- Hot glue

- Drill with a small bit

- Wire cutters

Drill a hole for the wire into the top of each log and the bottom of each pinecone. Stick the wire into the hole in the log, then stick the pinecone on the other end of the wire. If necessary, trim the wire with wire cutters. You can also reinforce the wire with a drop of hot glue.

Wrap the felt ribbon around the log several times and tie it in the front. Attach the buttons and twigs to the knot.

Use the hole punch to punch out four stars from the construction paper. Glue the stars onto the twigs.

Pine trees have a strong mythological significance. The Celts considered them to be holy, symbolizing the connection between heaven and earth. They also stood for protection and purity.

Christmas bakery scene

nostalgic fragrances

Total height

approx. 6 in. (15 cm)

Materials

- Old pie tin, 10 in. (25 cm) in diameter
- Corrugated packing cardboard
- Raffia
- Star anise
- Hazelnuts in the shell
- Shelled almonds
- Cinnamon sticks
- Dried orange slices
- Heather (or other dried herbs)
- Christmas cookies
- Apple
- Hot glue

Tear the corrugated packing cardboard into asymmetrical strips and roll them up into small cylinders, tying them with raffia. The cylinders are very easy to make if you wrap the corrugated cardboard around a container of the desired size, such as a glass or a jar.

Arrange the cardboard cylinders on the pie tin and attach them with hot glue.

Put the cinnamon sticks, orange peels and heather into the cylinders. Spread more cinnamon sticks, the nuts, the apple, and the star anise in the tin and glue them down. If you want, you can also add a few leftover cookies as decoration. The result is a charming Christmas greeting from your kitchen that also gives off an enchanting scent.

You might not find exactly the same pie tin, but that's all right. This idea works with almost any dish or pan that you can find while digging around your attic or at a flea market.

Pinecone star

a hanging Christmas greeting

Total height

12 in. (30 cm)

Materials

- Stretched canvas frame, 12 by 12 in. (30 by 30 cm)

- Corrugated-wire star, 10 in. (25 cm) in diameter

- Alder cones

- Red Christmas tree ornament, 2 in. (5 cm) in diameter

- Cardstock gift tag, 2 by 3 in. (5 by 8 cm)

- Rubber stamp with greeting

- Colorless stamp pad

- Gold embossing powder

- 16 in. (40 cm) red-and-white striped ribbon, ¼ in. (6 mm) wide

- Hot glue

- Heat gun (optional)

Attach the corrugated-wire star to the frame using hot glue; apply the glue to only a few spots. Next, glue the ornament in the center.

Fill in the star with the alder cones, applying a drop of hot glue to the underside of each small cone.

Next, stamp the Christmas greeting onto the gift tag. Dab the stamp *pad* onto the rubber *stamp* several times to coat it evenly (do not press the rubber stamp into the pad as you would with a normal stamp!). Sprinkle a generous amount of embossing powder onto the moist, stamped page and shake off the excess powder. If you shake it onto a sheet of paper and fold the paper, you can easily

pour the embossing powder back into the jar. If a few grains of powder stick to the paper around the writing, simply blow on the tag or remove them with a fine brush.

Use a heat gun to raise the stamping. Or hold the tag over a toaster, with the stamped writing facing up. The heat will melt the artificial resin powder to create a wonderfully shiny, sophisticated texture. The process is complete when the powder is no longer grainy. Remove it from the heat source at that point or the powder layer will flatten out.

Tie the ribbon to the ornament and the tag. Affix the tag to the frame with a drop of hot glue.

Slice of life

natural decorations

Total height

approx. 7½ in. (19 cm)

Materials

- Tree-trunk slice, 12 in. (30 cm) in diameter

- 6 small moss wreaths, 3 in. (8 cm) in diameter

- 9 branch slices, 2¾ to 4 in. (7 to 10 cm) in diameter

- Glass cylinders, 2½ in. (6.5 cm) in diameter, 3 in. (8 cm) tall

- Off-white pillar candles, 1½ in. (4 cm) in diameter, 2¼ in. (6 cm) tall

- Small round fir cones

- Pinecones

- Small wood slices as decoration

- 1½ yd. olive green and off-white plaid ribbon with wire edges, ⅞ in. (2.2 cm) wide

- Hot glue

- Decorating tape, if necessary

Arrange all of the elements on the tree-trunk slice and then glue them down using hot glue.

Make the candles different heights by gluing together different combinations of moss wreaths and branch slices. For the two candles in the back, use three branch slices and two moss wreaths each. For the center candle, use two branch slices and one moss wreath, and for the short candle in the front, use one branch slice and one moss wreath. Finish each stack with a branch slice.

Place the glass cylinders and candles on the branch slices. If a cylinder sits crooked, use decorating tape to adjust one of the lower layers (rather than placing the tape directly under the glass).

Finally, tie a length of plaid ribbon around the bottom of each glass cylinder.

This candle arrangement is a wonderful alternative to a traditional Advent wreath, but the individual stacks with the candles on top are also lovely on their own. You can use them as table decorations individually.

Magical winter stars

sparkle all the way

Total height

approx. 22 in. (55 cm)

Materials

- Empty food can, label removed

- Plaster powder

- Birch branch, 1 in. (2.5 cm), 20 in. (50 cm) long

- Sawdust

- 14 yd. (12.8 m) annealed winding wire

- 10 birchbark or paper stars, 2 in. (5 cm) in diameter

- 10 silver jingle bells, ¾ in. (19 mm) in diameter

- 16 small thick red wooden stars, 1 in. (2.5 cm) in diameter

- Larger thick wooden star, 2 in. (5 cm) in diameter

- 2 yd. (1.8 m) red-and-white plaid ribbon, ¼ in. (6 mm) wide

- Hot glue

- Staple gun

Fill the can about three-quarters full with water. To determine the exact volume of water, pour the water into a measuring cup and back into the can. Use the manufacturer's instructions to determine the necessary amount of plaster powder. Pour the powder into the can and stir well. Depending on the product, the plaster will take 15 to 30 minutes to harden. Once it starts to firm up, place the branch in the can and hold it upright or prop it up until the plaster is hard enough to hold it up alone. Let the mixture harden completely.

Take five pieces of winding wire and twist them together. The best way to do this is with another person, each inserting a stick or wooden spoon into a loop on the end and twisting the strand in opposite directions.

Next, attach the prepared wire to the back of the birch branch in several places, using the staple gun. It should form a nice spiral around the branch. The back of the object will be flat, so it will work best against a wall or in a niche.

Attach all of the stars with hot glue and tie the bells onto the wire with the ribbon. Finally, attach the large star and a bow with long ends to the top, using hot glue. Glue a wooden star to each end of the ribbon. Cover the surface of the plaster inside the can by spreading sawdust over it.

A creative Christmas season

natural materials in simple frames

Total height

8 in. (20 cm)/10 in. (27 cm)

Materials

- Papier-mâché or wood picture frames, 8 by 8 in. (20 by 20 cm) and 10 by 10 in. (27 by 27 cm)

- Matte white spray paint

- 28-gauge (0.3 mm) copper wire

- Light-brown leather-finish paper, 4 by 4 in. (10 by 10 cm) or 6 by 6 in. (15 by 15 cm)

- Gold glitter paper

- Tracing paper

- Assorted natural materials: fir cones, cinnamon sticks, sweetgum pods, poppy pods, reeds, rattan balls, and so on

- Star-shaped hole punches, 1 in. (2.5 cm) and 2½ in. (6.5 cm) in diameter

- Craft glue

- Hot glue

- Gold paint pen with 2–4 mm tip

First, coat the two picture frames with the spray paint. If you only apply one coat, the surface will be slightly transparent, and the uneven effect will make it look more lively.

Once the paint is dry, attach the two pieces of leather-finish paper to the backgrounds, using craft glue. Glue the various natural materials to the paper with hot glue to create a collage. It is a good idea to position the materials first before gluing them down. When it comes to natural materials, it is worth making sure the positioning is right.

Next, wrap the wire around the frames. Use the hole punches to punch out stars, which you can slide in between the wires and attach using a little craft glue if necessary.

Center your text on the tracing paper. If you like, you can make a template by printing out the text and placing it under the tracing paper. Then all you have to do is trace it with the paint pen. Fold down the edges of the piece of tracing paper and attach it to the frame with a small amount of craft glue.

Fence-post Saint Nicholas

adorable Santas made from simple materials

Total height

approx. 16 in. (40 cm)

Materials

- Small wooden fence posts, 2½ in. (6.5 cm) in diameter, 12 in. (30 cm) tall

- Modeling compound

- Palette knife

- 8 in. (20 cm) fine jute twine

- Natural wood balls without holes, ¾ in. (15 mm) in diameter

- Off-white yarn, medium thickness

- U.S. size J-10 (6.0 mm) crochet hook

- Red felt, two pieces measuring 8 by 12 in. (20 by 30 cm) each

- 2 round red Christmas-tree ornaments, 1½ in. (4 cm) in diameter

- 12 in. (30 cm) red satin ribbon, ⅛ in. (3 mm) wide

- Hot glue

- White glue

Clean any dirt off of the fence posts and use the palette knife to apply modeling compound for the beard. Give your creativity free rein here. Do you prefer it fluffy or narrow, curly or straight? If you would rather not apply the compound freehand, you can draw in the beard shape with a pencil first.

You can make the felt shapeable by dipping it in a 50/50 mixture of white glue and water. You want the piece wet but not dripping, so you might need to squeeze it gently. To create the hats, you can shape the wet felt by hand, twisting it into a point, and attaching it to the top of the posts. When it dries, it will harden enough to retain its shape.

For each eye, tie a knot in the middle of a short piece of twine. Attach the eyes and the nose—a natural wood ball—with hot glue.

Use the yarn to crochet a long chain. Glue two or three lengths of the crochet chain around the edge of the hat with the back side of the chain facing out for the "fur" trim. Finally, use the satin ribbon to attach the Christmas ornament to the end of the hat.

This is a great project to do with children. When kids are involved, applying the modeling compound and shaping the felt can get messy—but the whimsical results will be worth it. Craft projects like this are a great way to spend the days of Christmas vacation together. That long wait for Santa Claus will go by in the blink of an eye!

Having a ball

a unique Christmas tree

Total height

approx. 30 in. (80 cm)

Materials

- Pine or poplar board, 3½ in. (9 cm) wide, 16 in. (40 cm) long

- 2 pine or poplar boards, each 2¼ in. (6 cm) wide, 30 in. (78 cm) long

- 2 small corner braces

- 4 matching screws for the braces

- Hammer

- Wool felt, 2.5 in. (6.5 cm) wide, 3 in. (8 cm) long

- Various round decorations, e.g. rattan balls, vine balls, round Christmas-tree ornaments, Styrofoam balls (wrapped in yarn, twine, string, newspaper, copper wire, and so on)

- Fir cones

- Screwdriver

- Hot glue

Attach the corner braces to the wider board with the screws, about 2 in. (5 cm) from the edges. Then use a hammer to bend the braces inward so that when you attach the narrower boards to the braces on the base, they will slant inward and touch at their tips, forming a triangle. You do not need to be too precise when screwing them on or bending the braces—any impreciseness will disappear once you're finished.

Glue one end of the wool felt to the top edges of the two slats. Use plenty of glue, since this step will hold the slats together. Next, roll up the loose piece of the wool felt strip and attach the finished roll with a little hot glue.

Lay the triangle down on your work surface. You can slide the floorboard out past the edge of the table so that the frame lies flat. Start by loosely arranging your round objects in the frame. Once you are happy with the positioning, glue all of the parts to the frame and to each other using the hot glue. Try to create a three-dimensional effect. It is helpful to use small Christmas ornaments to cover up larger gaps between other objects.

Festive candlelight

enchantingly decorated with star anise

Total height

approx. 8 in. (20 cm)

Materials

- Natural-colored paper bag, 9 by 12 in. (23 by 30 cm), base width: 4 in. (10 cm)
- 2 yd. (1.8 m) natural wool yarn
- 1½ yd. (1.4 m) natural twisted paper ribbon
- 28-gauge (0.3 mm) copper wire
- Cardstock gift tag, 2 by 3 in. (5 by 8 cm)
- Package twine, approx. 12 in. (30 cm)
- Star anise
- Champagne-colored metallic paper, 3 by 3 in. (8 by 8 cm)
- White pillar candle, 2¼ in. (6 cm) in diameter, 3 in. (8 cm) tall
- Matching glass hurricane
- Craft glue

Cut the handles off the paper bag, if needed. Next, carefully crumple the bag and roll the top edge down slightly.

To make the bag a little more stable, add the glass cylinder at this stage. Tie knots in the yarn at irregular intervals, wrap it loosely around the bag below the folded-down lip, and tie the ends together. Untwist the paper ribbon in a few places, wrap it around your finger, and then drape it around the bag.

Use the copper wire and star anise to make a chain, wrapping the wire around the star anise pieces. Position the pods at irregular intervals, but not too far apart. Tie the finished chain around the bag.

Cut a star out of the construction paper, glue it to the center of the gift tag, and attach the star anise with copper wire as shown. Use the package twine to tie the finished tag to your bag.

Star anise is especially popular for baking and decorating during the Christmas season. It is especially appropriate for the holidays because of its star shape. Star anise has eight semi-open pods that radiate out from the center, each revealing a smooth, shining, red-brown seed.

Little friends for a chilly season

make a bit of magic

Total height

approx. 13 to 24 in. (33 to 61 cm)

Materials, general

- Plaster bandages
- Hot glue
- Different sizes of fire logs

Materials for the Santa

- 3 pieces of cardboard: 1 circle 6¼ in. (16 cm) in diameter, 2 rectangles 8¼ by 9 in. (21 by 23 cm) and 2½ by 14 in. (6 by 35 cm)
- Natural wood ball without a hole, ¾ in. (20 mm) in diameter
- 2 natural wood buttons, ¾ in. (18 mm) in diameter
- Fine jute twine
- 9 yd. (8.2 m) medium-weight off-white yarn (twisted into a cord)
- Thick red felt, 6½ by 7 in. (17 by 18 cm)

Materials for the Reindeer

- 4 pieces of cardboard: 8¼ by 8½ in. (21 by 22 cm), 9 by 17 in. (23 by 43 cm), 2½ by 14 in. (6 by 35 cm), and 1½ by 2½ in. (4 by 6 cm) (for the nose)
- 2 natural wood buttons, ¾ in. (18 mm) in diameter
- Fine jute twine
- Approx. 1 yd. (0.9 m) medium-weight red yarn
- Small amount (less than 1 yd. [0.9 m]) fine red-and-white yarn
- 3 round Christmas ornaments, 1½ in. (4 cm) in diameter
- 2 stars made of birchbark or paper, 1¾ in. (4.5 cm) in diameter

Materials for the Winter Child

- 2 pieces of cardboard: 1 circle 6¼ in. (16 cm) in diameter and 1 rectangle 2½ by 14 in. (6 by 35 cm)
- 2 natural wood buttons, ¾ in. (18 mm) in diameter
- Natural wood ball, ⅝ in. (15 mm) in diameter, cut in half
- Fine jute twine

- 1 yd. (0.9 m) worsted-weight yarn in red and off-white
- U.S. size J-10 (6.0 mm) crochet hook
- Pom-pom kit, if desired, for a pom-pom with a diameter of 2 in. (5 cm)
- Hat label
- Branch
- White ramie ribbon, ⅜ in. (1 cm) wide
- 28-gauge (0.3 mm) silver craft wire

Materials for the Snowman

- 3 pieces of cardboard: 1 circle 6¼ in. (16 cm) in diameter, 2 rectangles 6 by 10 in. (15 by 26 cm) and 10 by 14 in. (6 by 35 cm)
- 12 in. (30 cm) plaid linen ribbon, 1½ in. (4 cm) wide
- 2 natural wood buttons, ¾ in. (18 mm) in diameter
- Sweetgum pod
- Fine and medium jute twine
- 2 yd. (1.8 m) red worsted-weight yarn
- U.S. size 10 (6.0 mm) knitting needles

Patterns

Pages 62–63

Note: The samples shown here were made with myboshi yarn (30% merino superwash wool, 70% acrylic), in red (132) and ivory (192).

33

The four variations are all put together in the same way.

I covered all of the white cardboard pieces with plaster bandages, cutting the bandages into convenient sizes. Since it can be dusty work, I recommend cutting them over an empty box to catch the plaster dust.

Quickly dip each piece into a bowl of water and place it on the cardboard. Make sure no water drips onto the unused plaster pieces, since there is no way to soften plaster once it has hardened. The plaster will harden fairly fast, but it needs a few hours to dry completely. Until it is done hardening, the cardboard may need a little support because it has been softened by the water. But you can also shape it however you like during this time. For instance, the reindeer antlers are more expressive if you curve them a bit rather than leaving them completely flat.

Cut the cardboard strip specified in the material list with the corrugated lines running lengthwise to make sure it provides enough stability. Fold the cardboard into a triangle by making three evenly spaced folds in it and gluing the two end sections to each other with hot glue. The triangle lets you determine the angle of the head. Glue the resulting stand to the top of the log with hot glue, then attach the head pieces to the cardboard triangle.

Wood buttons are used as eyes for all of the figures. Thread the jute string through the holes and tie it in the back, then attach the prepared buttons to the faces with hot glue.

For the accessories, such as the scarf, the hat, and the folded stars, you can craft, knit, or crochet whatever you want; of course, you can also use ready-made items. Let your imagination run free and make whatever you feel like.

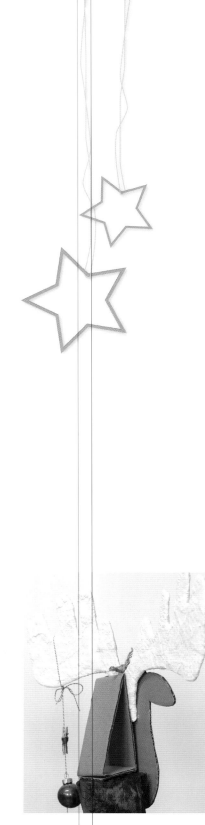

A simple piece of cardboard is used to support the head.

A cheerful wall decoration

in enchanting, Christmasy red

Total height

approx. 48 in. (122 cm)

Materials

- 4 vine bouquet forms, 6 in. (15 cm) and 8 in. (20 cm) in diameter

- Driftwood pieces

- 2 yd. (1.8 m) red gingham ribbon, ⅝ in. (15 mm) wide

- 1 yd. (0.9 m) red gingham ribbon, ⅜ in. (10 mm) wide

- 2 yd. (1.8 m) red satin ribbon, ¼ in. (6 mm) wide

- 3½ yd. (3.2 m) red yarn

- 7 red felt stars, 2 in. (5 cm) in diameter

- 15 thick white wooden stars, 1 in. (2.5 cm) and 1½ in. (4 cm) in diameter

- Hot glue

- Wire cutters

Bouquet forms consist of a metal frame surrounded by vines or other natural materials. Florists use them for floral arrangements.

Start by trimming off the wire pieces from the bouquet forms so that you can use the pretty vine part.

Connect the vine circles with the gingham ribbon to make a chain.

Next, attach the decorative elements to the individual vine circles with hot glue.

Christmas with flair

a standing collage made from natural materials

Total height

approx. 36 in. (91 cm)

Materials

- Firewood log, approx. 5 in. (13 cm) wide, 9 in. (23 cm) tall
- Willow rod
- 5 birchbark or paper squares, 4 by 4 in. (10 by 10 cm)
- 6 birchbark or paper stars, 2 in. (5 cm) in diameter
- Green craft grass
- Various seed pods
- Dried lemon slices
- Moss
- Small matte red mirrored balls
- Various ribbons
- Hot glue
- Drill with bit same diameter as the willow rod

Start by drilling the holes in the log and the birchbark squares and stars.

Next, place the craft grass on the log, covering the top. Remove any excess material. Uncover the hole in the top of the log and stick the willow rod into it. Fix it in place with hot glue if needed.

Now carefully thread a birchbark square onto the rod. Glue a layer of small seed pods to the birchbark, then add another birchbark square. Repeat the process with the lemon slices, moss, mirrored balls, and dried star-fruit. Finish with one more birchbark square.

Thread the birchbark stars onto the willow rod and tie the ribbons to the end of the rod. Glue two stars to the front and back of the knots.

This decoration can be made with any combination of natural materials. Dried poppy pods, small fir cones, acorns, cinnamon sticks, and dried moss would all work. On your next walk in the woods, or trip to the florist or craft store, keep your eyes open.

Star mail

a simple display for your Christmas cards

Total height

approx. 5 ft. (1.5 m)

Materials

- Board made of pine or poplar, 7 by 12 in. (18 by 30 cm)
- Pine or poplar board for the vertical, 8 by 50 in. (20 cm by 1.3 m)
- 2 metal L brackets
- 4 matching screws for the brackets
- Natural vine wreath, 12 in. (30 cm) in diameter
- 5½ yd. (5 m) olive-green felt ribbon, ½ in. (1.3 cm) wide
- 15 natural thick wooden stars, 1½ in. (4 cm) and 2 in. (5 cm) in diameter
- 10 magnets, ½ in. (1.2 cm) in diameter, and 10 magnets that stick to them (20 total)
- Cardboard, 3 by 3 in. (8 by 8 cm) and 1½ by 2¼ in. (4 by 6 cm)
- Olive-green and off-white yarn, worsted weight
- U.S. size J-10 (6.0 mm) crochet hook
- White, green, and plaid ribbons
- Hot glue
- Cordless drill

First, attach the base board to the main piece with the two brackets and screws. Wrap the felt ribbon tightly around the board as shown, and attach the ends to the back with hot glue. Attach the wreath and five of the wooden stars with hot glue as well. The rest of the stars will be used to hold your Christmas cards. Glue the magnets to the stars with hot glue. Their opposites will be glued onto the board as backing, so you can attach the cards either by sliding them under the felt ribbon or by sticking them on with a magnetic star.

Cut out a freehand flame from the smaller piece of cardboard and wrap it in white yarn. Use the green yarn to crochet a tube made of 24 stitches in half double crochet, and slide the other piece of cardboard into it. Attach the finished candle to the wreath with hot glue. Finally, tie the short ribbon pieces and yarn pieces to the vine wreath.

You can replace the decorative candle with any other decorative element if, unlike me, you haven't caught the crocheting bug. One possible alternative I had was a fabric doll with dangling legs, which I liked almost as much.

Total height

approx. 48 in. (122 cm)

Materials

- Pine wood slab, approx. 10 in. (25 cm) wide and 48 in. (122 cm) long

- Thin (approx. ¾ in. [1.9 cm]) board, 1 yd. (0.9 m) long

- Hinge with matching screws

- Wooden block, 3 by 4 by 4 in. (8 by 10 by 10 cm)

- 2 screws in the right length for the wooden block

- Sage green wool yarn

- 8 cream-colored felt stars, 2 in. (5 cm) in diameter

- 1 yd. (0.9 m) dark brown jute ribbon, 1½ in. (4 cm) wide

- Gold leaf (or gold paint)

- Adhesive for the gold leaf

- Brush to apply the leaf adhesive

- Flat brush

- String (10 to 20 in. [25 to 51 cm])

Star over Bethlehem

an impressive standing display

- Glass jar, 3½ in. (9 cm) in diameter, 8 in. (20 cm) tall
- Large cream-colored tea light
- Coffee beans
- Hot glue
- Drill
- Jigsaw
- Large nail or old knife
- Screwdriver, manual or cordless

Pattern

Page 61

Transfer the star pattern to one end of the board and cut out the top three points with the jigsaw. Cut a groove around the bottom two points with a nail or an old knife to make the edges deeper.

Coat the star with the gold leaf: First, apply a thick layer of adhesive and let it dry slightly according to the manufacturer's instructions. Clean the brush with water right away. Once the drying period is over, place the gold leaf on the surface, press it down with the flat brush and shake off any excess. Place a piece of paper underneath to catch the extra pieces, which can be reused. (Instead of leafing, you can paint the star gold.)

You can also put other natural materials into the jar—for instance, dried orange slices. When choosing the other decorative elements, you can coordinate them with the colors of the natural materials you have used.

Attach the wooden block with two screws. Pre-drill the holes through the board, which is fairly thick.

In order for your display to stand freely, screw the hinge onto the back side of the board and to the end of the roof lath. You can adjust the angle by attaching a piece of string to the bottom third of the hinge. The string will keep the roof lath from opening wider than you want it to.

Next, attach the decorative elements. Wrap the jute ribbon around the board and tie it. Wrap the yarn around the board several times and tie that, too. Place four felt stars underneath it and affix them with hot glue. Decorate the wooden block by attaching the jute ribbon and yarn with hot glue.

Wrap the yarn around the glass jar several times and tie the ends. Attach the remaining felt stars with hot glue. Finally, fill the jar with coffee beans and add the tea light. The jar is simply set on the wooden block.

Pure nature

a lovingly detailed doorman

Total height

approx. 60 in. (152 cm)

Materials

- Large empty can, label removed
- Plaster
- Moss
- Straight branch
- Green raffia
- 28-gauge (0.3 mm) silver craft wire
- Small fir cones
- Larger fir cones
- Pine needle bunches
- Moss wreaths, 3in. (8 cm) and 5 in. (13 cm) in diameter
- Silver upholstery nails
- Star-shaped hole punch, 1 in. (2.5 cm) in diameter
- Mulberry paper, newspaper, and vellum paper
- Natural-colored wool yarn
- Vine ball, 6 in. (15 cm) in diameter
- Bleached rattan ball, 2¾ in. (7 cm) in diameter
- 20 in. (50 cm) olive-green wool yarn
- 5½ yd. (5 m) olive-green herringbone ribbon, ⅜ in. (10 mm) wide
- Hot glue

Fill the can about three-quarters full with water. To determine the exact volume of water, pour the water into a measuring cup and back into the can. Use the manufacturer's instructions to determine the necessary amount of plaster powder. Pour the powder into the can and stir well. Depending on the product, the plaster will take 15 to 30 minutes to harden. Once it starts to firm up, place the branch in the can and hold it upright or prop it up until the plaster is hard enough to hold it up alone. Let the plaster harden completely.

Attach the decorative elements to the branch with hot glue or by tying them on with the yarn, plaid ribbon, or wire.

Punch stars out of the papers and attach them to the large moss wreath with the upholstery nails. Attach the wreath to the branch, using the plaid ribbon.

Finally, use the moss to cover the plaster surface in the can.

With this project, I wanted to show you an easy way to make large, beautiful decorative pieces. If you enjoy making it, you can also make several small ones, for instance, for your windowsill—or even smaller ones for table decorations. The base can always be a can filled with plaster.

A bag of light

fascinating shadow plays

Total height

approx. 4 in. (10 cm)

Materials

- Paper sandwich bags
- Glass containers, 3 in. (8 cm) in diameter, 2¾ in. (7 cm) tall
- Hole punches in various shapes, 1 in. (3 cm) in diameter
- Green raffia
- Small wood slices, 1 in. (2.5 cm) in diameter
- Olive-green glitter paper
- Double-sided foam adhesive tape
- Double-sided adhesive tape
- Drill with ¹⁄₁₀ in. (3 mm) bit

These little treasures also make nice little presents. Everyone is enchanted when the candle is lit and the motifs glued to the inside of the bag shine through.

Use a hole punch to punch out several copies of your chosen motif from a bag, then glue the individual pieces around the glass, using double-sided tape.

Carefully roll up the edge of another bag and place the prepared glass inside, with a tea light in it.

Drill a small hole in a wood slice. Punch the motif out of the glitter paper and attach it to the slice with a piece of foam tape. Wrap the raffia around the bag and tie it to the slice of wood.

Winter white

surrounded by stars

Total height

approx. 8 in. (20 cm)

Materials

- White paper shopping or gift bag, 9 by 12 in. (23 by 30 cm), base width: 4 in. (10 cm)

- 2 yd. (1.8 m) olive-green wool yarn

- Heavy vellum or similar paper

- Star-shaped hole punch, 1½ in. (4 cm) in diameter

- Hole punch, ¹/₁₀ in. (3 mm) in diameter

- Clematis branches, total of approx. 2 yd. (1.8 m)

- Brown craft wire

- White pillar candle, 2½ in. (6 cm) in diameter, 3 in. (8 cm) tall

- Matching hurricane cylinder

- Craft glue

Start by cutting the handles off the paper bag if it has them. Next, carefully crumple the bag and roll up the top edge slightly.

To make the bag a little more stable, add the glass cylinder at this stage. Wrap the yarn around the bag below the folded-down lip and tie the ends together. Next, wrap the clematis loosely around the bag and tie the ends with craft wire. You can also use the wire to attach pieces of vine or adjust the shape if necessary.

Punch several stars out of the vellum. Hang the stars on the thin tendrils of the vine, as shown in the photo. Make the holes with the hole punch, adjusting the diameter to the thickness of the tendrils. Save a few stars without any holes and attach them directly to the vine or the bag with a little bit of craft glue.

The vine wreath also looks very festive without the paper bag. Make it as described above; for this version, I used slightly longer vines to give it a fuller look. Then simply set the candle in the center of the wreath.

Forest creatures

benevolent spirits in a nutshell

Total height

approx. 3 to 4 in. (8 to 10 cm)

Materials

- Walnuts
- Dried trumpet mushrooms
- Thin red cord
- Gold jingle bells, ½ in. (12 mm) in diameter
- 30-gauge (0.25 mm) copper wire
- Hot glue

These fun little sprites not only make adorable Christmas tree ornaments, they can also be used as creative gift tags.

You can quickly and easily make charming Christmas sprites out of dried trumpet mushrooms and walnuts. To hang them up, attach a loop of copper wire to the mushroom stem before you wrap the cord around the stem; the unattractive end is then hidden by the cord.

Simply wrap the cord around the stem of the trumpet mushrooms. The length will depend on the size of each mushroom. When tying the cord ends, also attach the jingle bell.

Finally, you need the head to go with the hat. Use hot glue to attach a walnut inside each mushroom.

Angel with a heart

a heavenly guardian

Total height

approx. 9 in. (23 cm)

Materials

- Small round wooden pointed post, 2 in. (5 cm) in diameter, 12 in. (30 cm) tall

- Dense cotton ball, 2 in. (5 cm) in diameter

- 30 in. (76 cm) medium-weight jute twine

- 48 in. (122 cm) 12-gauge (2 mm) silver aluminum wire

- Gray decorative heart, 2 in. (5 cm) wide

- Staple gun

- Round-nose pliers

- Hot glue

The cotton ball will be the angel's head. Make a hole in the cotton ball that is big enough for the ball to fit on the point of the fence post. Use a little hot glue to make sure it stays in place.

Shape a piece of the jute string into a round halo and attach it to the angel's head with a drop of hot glue.

Bend the aluminum wire into a decorative wing shape as shown here. You can use the round-nose pliers to create beautiful curves. Attach the finished wings to the back of the fence post using the staple gun. Finally, tie the heart to the other piece of jute string and hang it around your angel's neck, gluing it in place if needed.

Winter tales

for cozy evenings by the fireside

Total height

approx. 8 in. (20 cm)

Materials

- Old hardcover books
- White acrylic paint
- Flat brush
- 2 yd. (1.8 m) gray plaid ribbon, ³⁄₈ in. (10 mm) wide
- Pine needles
- Branches or pieces of bark
- Whitewashed wooden star, approx. 4 in. (10 cm) in diameter, ³⁄₄ in. (2 cm) thick
- Flat wooden stars, approx. 1½ in. (3.5 cm) in diameter
- Star-shaped hole punch, 1 in. (2.5 cm) in diameter
- White feathers
- 30-gauge (0.25 mm) silver wire
- Pillar candle, 3 in. (8 cm) in diameter, 4 in. (10 cm) tall
- Hot glue
- Decorating tape

First, remove the dust jacket and tear a page out of one of the books. Then coat the books in acrylic paint. The books may need two coats of paint. Let the paint dry completely.

Glue the books together in a decorative arrangement, as shown, and tie them with the plaid ribbon. Do not trim the long ends of the ribbon.

Bundle the pine needles together with the silver wire; wrap the ends of the feathers in wire, too.

Position the candle as shown and hold it in place with decorating tape. Arrange the branches or bark pieces diagonally on the stack of books and glue them down.

Decorate with all of the other elements as desired and glue everything down.

Finally, punch some stars out of the torn-out page and attach them. If you like, you can curl the stars a bit, to make them more lively and sculptural.

You can make all kinds of creative objects out of old, unused books. If you have a large number of books handy, you can make tall, free-standing pedestals or a long frieze with many more candles. A taller stack with offset books also creates small ledges where you can set decorations. And a single book can make an original little present!

Cold-weather preserves

capturing the season in jars

Total height

approx. 12 in. (30 cm)

Materials

- Various glass jars with lids

- Off-white pillar candles in matching sizes

- Various natural materials for filling the jars: tinder, fir cones, cinnamon sticks, dried orange slices, nuts, and so on.

- Dark-brown satin ribbon with small star pattern, ³/₈ in. (10 mm) wide

- Green wire stars, 1 to 2 in. (2.5 to 5 cm) in diameter

After Christmas, you can fill the jars with other decorative materials depending on the time of year. Non-seasonal decorations, such as corks or pretty stones, can also be decorative.

Fill the jars with the natural materials. They look especially interesting if you layer the various materials on top of one another.

Tie a satin ribbon around each jar and attach it to a wire star. Put a lid on the jar and place the pillar candle on it.

As good as gold

a chic hanging decoration

Total height

approx. 43 in. (110 cm)

Materials

- 2 yd. (1.8 m) off-white wool yarn
- Dried passionfruit
- Dried leaves
- Vine ball, 3 in. (8 cm) in diameter
- Champagne-colored angel-hair (spun glass decoration)
- 30-gauge (0.25 mm) copper wire
- Small brushwood wreath, 3 in. (8 cm) in diameter
- Cinnamon sticks
- Dried apple slices
- Pinecones
- Miniature wooden clothes-pins, 2 in. (5 cm) long
- Off-white tissue paper or transparent paper, 2½ by 11 in. (6 by 28 cm)
- Gold gel pen with a 0.6 mm point
- Gold-colored aluminum foil

Start by threading all the large elements onto the yarn or tying them to one another. You may need to drill holes in some of the materials in order to hang them. Simple overhand knots will keep the individual elements separate. Finish off the strand with the pinecone.

Once you are happy with the way the chain looks, add the other decorations, like the gold wire, the angelhair, and the stars made from the gold foil.

Use the gel pen to write a Christmas message on the transparent paper, and attach it to the yarn with the wooden clothespin.

You can use this method to make very long chains. Despite its soft appearance, yarn is very durable. I like to hang this type of chain in a tall, narrow window next to my balcony door, or on the support post in my kitchen.

Precious guardian angels

handsome good-luck charms for the whole year

Total height

approx. 1½ in. (4 cm)

Materials

- Semiprecious stone beads, approx. ½ in. (13 mm) and ¾ in. (19 mm) in diameter

- Silver head pins, 2½ in. (6 cm) long

- Wing jewelry elements, approx. 1 in. (2.5 cm) wide

- Bead caps, ½ in. (13 mm) in diameter

- Miniature bead caps, ¹⁄₁₀ in. (4 mm) in diameter

- 28-gauge (0.3 mm) silver jewelry wire

- Round-nose pliers

- Flat-nose pliers

Thread all of the pieces of the angel onto the eye pin—first the miniature bead cap, then the large semiprecious bead, the wings, the small semi-precious bead, and finally the large bead cap. Use the round-nose pliers to bend the top of the eye pin into a loop. You can thread the jewelry wire through the loop to use it as a pendant.

These little guardian angels make wonderful gift tags and small, very personal presents. Semiprecious stones are said to contain special energy that flows into the wearer.

Agate Protection and safety, grants inner strength, reduces stress.

Amber Drives away sad thoughts, promotes patience.

Jade Stands for harmony and peace, promotes restful sleep and pleasant dreams.

Lapis lazuli Promotes self-confidence, reduces fears and the feeling of uncertainty.

Malachite Stimulates the desire for adventure, inspires the imagination and powers of decision.

Onyx Stands for endurance, single-mindedness, and convincing argumentation.

Quartz Clarity of thought, positive energy.

Rose quartz Increases empathy, promotes happiness in love.

Tiger's eye Helps keep a clear head, promotes concentration, and calms the nerves.

Turquoise Protects the wearer from outside influences, helps sharpen intuition about one's own life and body.

O Christmas tree

without any needles to sweep up

Total height

approx. 22 in. (56 cm)

Materials

- Various rough pieces of branches

- Medium-weight jute string

- Round red Christmas ornaments, 1 in. (2.5 cm) in diameter

- Round red Christmas ornament, 1½ in. (4 cm) in diameter

- Hot glue

Lay out your branches on the table and arrange them into the shape of a Christmas tree. Take advantage of the unique characteristics of the individual pieces. That's what makes every tree a fascinating, one-of-a-kind object! You will find that it's easy to put together if you have a large selection of branches and twigs.

Tie the ends of the branches together with the jute string. To make sure the Christmas tree is stable, I also attach the branches to each other with hot glue before tying them.

Next, tie the smaller ornaments to the lower branch in a row, using the string. The single larger ornament is attached to the top.

No one knows where the custom of decorating an evergreen tree at Christmastime comes from. But over the centuries, it has become common all over the world. Hardly any other symbol is as closely linked with Christmas as the Christmas tree. Incidentally, the world's largest Christmas tree is not in New York, as many people believe, but at the Christmas market in Dortmund, Germany.

Advent, Advent

four candles herald the Christmas celebration

Total height

approx. 13 in. (34 cm)

Materials

- Log, approx. 6 in. (15 cm) wide, 24 in. (61 cm) long

- 4 candle holders, 3 in. (8 cm) in diameter

- 4 ivory candles, 2½ in. (6 cm) in diameter, 4 in. (10 cm) tall

- Branches from various evergreen trees

- Holly branches

- 5 dried banana (or other long) leaves

- Green winding wire

- Drill with a thin wood bit

- Hot glue

Make sure the log is dry and fairly clean. If necessary, drill four holes into the log to hold the candle holders. Be sure to leave a slightly larger space between the two middle holes. The bundle of branches will go here later on.

Next, stick the candle holders into the predrilled holes. Or you can use a little hot glue to attach them and keep them steady.

Combine the branches and the leaves into a nice arrangement. Tie the materials together in the middle with the winding wire.

Try to hide the wire under the branches as much as possible so that it isn't too noticeable.

Lay the bundle across the log between the two middle candle holders. Finally, stick the white pillar candles into the candle holders.

If you want more decorations on your Advent table, you can scatter the other elements around the log. I can imagine using apples, individual Christmas ornaments, and of course pinecones. You can often find good, natural-looking decorative fruit in specialty stores, too. That gives you the option of highlighting this elegant but simple decoration with a little more color.

Bearded trio

three witty wedges

Total height

approx. 12 in. (30 cm)

Materials

- 3 wooden wedges, approx. 8 in. (20 cm) tall

- Matching natural wood balls, cut in half

- For the hats: felt strips in any color, 6 in. (15 cm) wide

- For the beards: off-white felt strips, 6 in. (15 cm) wide

- Fine nylon thread

- Hot glue

Pattern

Page 60

Choose three light-colored wooden wedges. Make sure the wedges can stand on a surface without wobbling. The upper end of each piece should be a little bit narrower than the base.

For the hat, wrap the felt band around a wedge. Cut the length to size. Then roll up the felt band and glue it together with a little hot glue to create a tube. Gather the fabric together at one end and tie it with the nylon thread to form a point. Repeat the process for the other two figures, then place the hats over the narrower ends of the wooden wedges.

Cut out the beard pieces from the white felt band, using the pattern provided. Gather the mustaches at the ends and in the middle as shown, and tie them with nylon thread.

Glue the natural wood balls just below the edge of the hat with hot glue, and attach the beards and mustaches.

Patterns

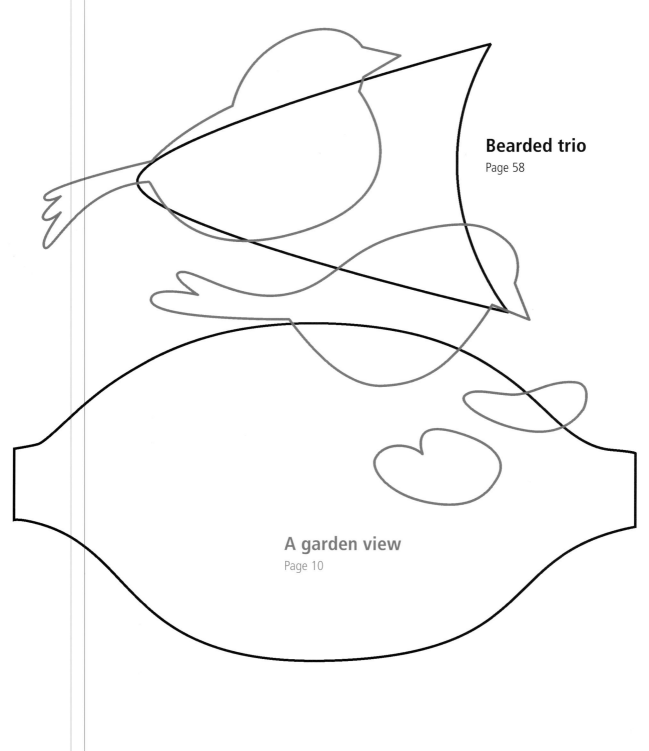

Bearded trio
Page 58

A garden view
Page 10

Star over Bethlehem
Enlarge pattern to 125%
Page 40

Little friends for a chilly season

Page 32

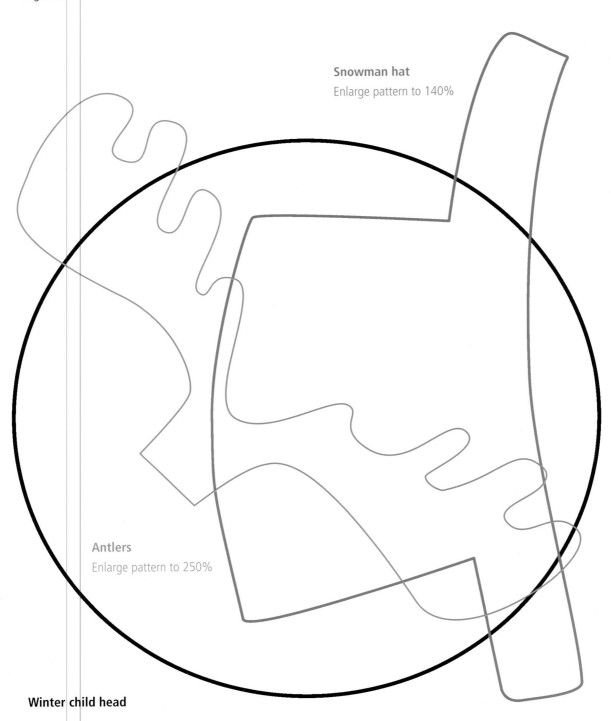

Snowman hat
Enlarge pattern to 140%

Antlers
Enlarge pattern to 250%

Winter child head

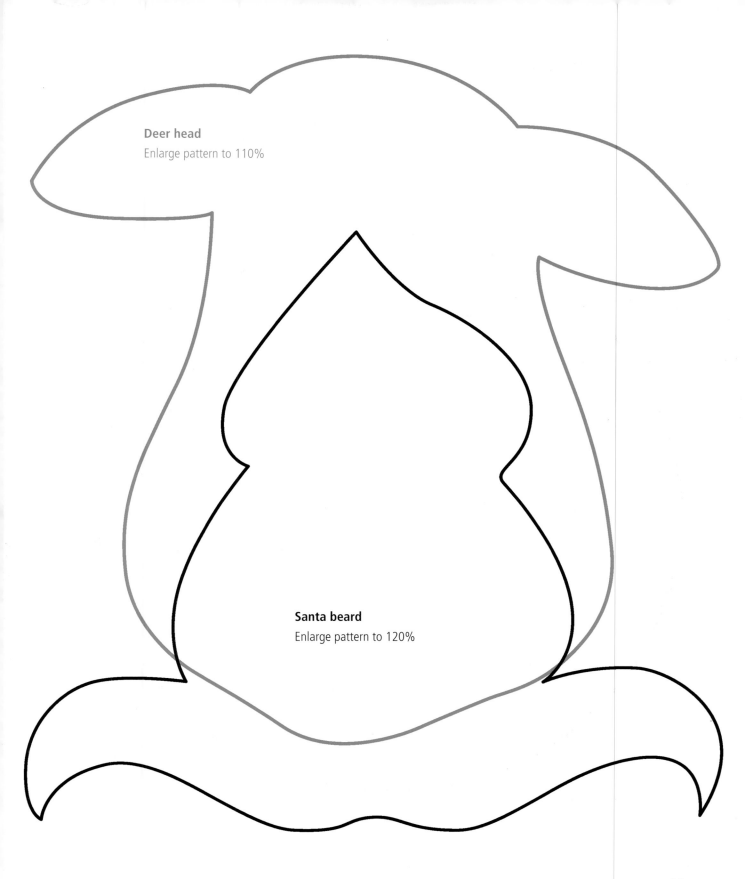

Deer head
Enlarge pattern to 110%

Santa beard
Enlarge pattern to 120%

About the author

Ilona Butterer is the brains, heart, and hands behind Creativ Markt Butterer in Bruchsal, Germany. Her two shops have become known well beyond the boundaries of this small city in Baden-Württemberg, and she also works nationally as a consultant and product developer. In addition to all of her entrepreneurial obligations, she always manages to find time for creative projects like this book. She is convinced that being creative is good for the soul, brings color to our everyday lives, and helps us practice taking things into our own hands.

Credits

PHOTOS: frechverlag GmbH, 70499 Stuttgart; Ilona Butterer (page 34); fotolia.de: Christian Jung (pages 2, 16, 30, 64), Cpro (page 21 right, 57 top), Daniel Ernst (page 2 bottom, 29), heigri (page 53 left), Ingo Sch. (page 54) Kaarsten (page 3 top, 6), LianeM (page 14), Marianne Mayer (page 1, 21 left, 33, 47, 58), michaklootwijk (page 18), Stauke (page 53 right), Sunnydays (page 8, 37), womue (page 27, 41); lichtpunkt, Michael Ruder, Stuttgart (all others)

PRODUCT MANAGEMENT: Mariel Marohn
LAYOUT AND EXECUTION: Heike Köhl, Katrin Krengel
TRANSLATION: Emily Banwell
COVER DESIGN: Tessa J. Sweigert

The original German edition of this book was published as *Natürlich schöne Weihnachtszeit*.
Copyright © 2013 frechverlag GmbH, Stuttgart, Germany (www.frech.de)
The author would like to thank Thomas Jaensich and Felix Roland from myboshi for permission to use their trademark on pages 32–33.
This edition is published by an arrangement with Claudia Böhme Rights & Literary Agency, Hannover, Germany (www.agency-boehme.com).
English edition copyright © 2014 by Stackpole Books

Published by Stackpole Books
5067 Ritter Road
Mechanicsburg, PA 17055
www.stackpolebooks.com

Printed in the United States of America
10 9 8 7 6 5 4 3 2 1
First edition

ISBN 978-0-8117-1431-0

Cataloging-in-Publication Data is on file with the Library of Congress.